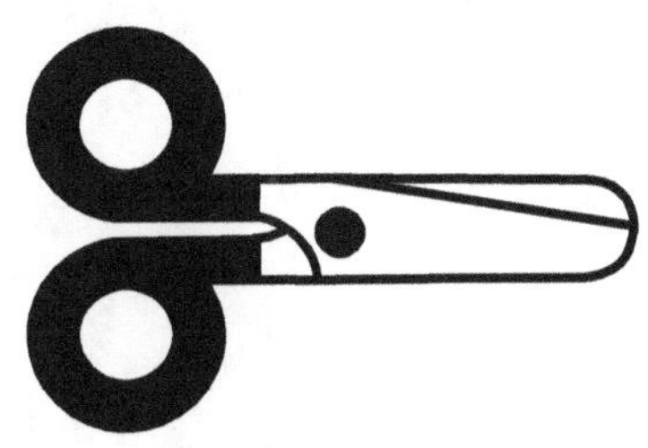

This Book Belongs To:

____

GO PLAY WITH JUNK!

A STEM Upcycling Activity Book for Boys and Girls

For Samuel

Table of Contents

Introduction

Have you checked your curiosity bone lately?
That's the part of you that wonders what's inside a
clock, how planes stay in the air, or whether you could
build something totally new from scraps? That spark
of wondering is what powers inventors, engineers, and
dreamers. It's the starting point for every "what if?" and
"why not?" that ever changed the world.

A Learner's Mindset
A learner's mindset starts with curiosity and ends with
critical thinking. This mindset is always asking 'why' and
figuring out 'how to make it better'.

The world's greatest inventors, scientists, and engineers
all started with a simple spark: curiosity. They asked bold
questions, took things apart, made mistakes, and kept
going.

In this book, you'll meet real-life STEM heroes who turned
their curiosity into world-changing ideas. They weren't
perfect people or genius know-it-alls. They started out as
curious kids who loved to tinker and explore.

So don't be afraid to ask "why," get messy, or take a risk.
Every experiment, mistake, and "aha!" moment is a step
toward becoming a maker, thinker, or problem-solver. Just
like them, you're built from curiosity and that's exactly
where big ideas begin.

Note to Grown-Ups:

This book invites kids to explore, experiment, and learn by doing. Step in to help only when they ask. Let them take the lead!

Encourage teamwork and creative problem-solving whenever possible. Have older children partner with younger ones, share their designs, and explain their ideas to others. Give kids the chance to be the teacher.

As long as it's safe, let them take charge of their STEM upcycling learning adventure.

Note to K-12 Teachers:

All activities in this book align with Next Generation Science Standards (NGSS) and promotes real-world problem solving through the engineering design process to imagine, build, test, and redesign.

Most of the activities take between 30 and 60 minutes to complete. They are perfect for afterschool programs, STEM clubs, makerspaces, and the like. The activities are flexible and can be incorporated in your STEM curriculum as it helps students explore physics, engineering, and environmental science while building confidence, creativity, and teamwork skills.

This book supports Common Core math and literacy connections through journaling and reflection prompts It's aligned with K-8 NGSS Engineering Design (ETS1) and Physical Science (PS2) standards.

Lastly, this book also supports the North Carolina Portrait of a Graduate, an educational framework that ensures students graduate equipped with the ability to adapt, to collaborate, communicate, think critically, show empathy, learn and take personal responsibility, whatever path they take in life.

Using This Book

Whether you're a classroom teacher, afterschool coordinator, librarian, or parent. This book is designed to make hands-on STEM simple and exciting for kids and easy for you to lead.

Start with What You Have
Most activities in this book use common household and recycled materials. Before buying anything, try collecting:
- Paper towel tubes, cereal boxes, string, rubber bands
- Bottle caps, plastic lids, paper scraps, cardboard
- Old buttons, scraps of fabric, plastic and metal containers

Leader Tip: Set up a "Upcycling Station" where kids can donate clean items during the week.

Keep It Flexible
The activities in this book are ideal for afterschool or out-of-school time. As you know, these times can be unpredictable. Kids may come and go, and sessions may run short.

Use the journaling sections and redesign prompts to stretch time. Let kids work at their own pace and in teams. Encourage creativity over perfection. Perfection in STEM is a myth, to be honest. Enjoy the STEM creation journey.

Guiding Principles

Redesign = Real Engineering
The first build usually isn't the best and that's great! Help kids:
- Test what worked (and didn't)
- Think of new ways to solve a problem
- Try again with different materials

Foster this STEM design mindset: Failure isn't the end. It's where learning begins!

The **Built From Curiosity** Spotlights are included to show how real STEM people started out as curious kids. Use the ones in this book or create your own about other STEM professionals.

Guide. Don't solve.
Guidance is required. Solutions are not.
Be curious with the kids. Ask questions. Encourage trying, tinkering, and testing.

Build with Purpose
Upcycling is an act of empathy. You're showing care for our planet. Who is this invention for? or How could this design help someone or our community? Your tinkering can have bigger purpose.

Focus on exploration, not explanation.

The Authors

Claude and Linda Hargrove's story began at NC State University, where they were both studying engineering. They shared a love for science, technology, and solving problems. These interests had sparked their curiosity since childhood.

Dr. Claude M. Hargrove / Linda Hargrove, M.S.

Over time, those shared passions led them to careers in engineering and to their work as parents and mentors.

Claude earned degrees in Computer, Electrical, and Biological Engineering, working in both industry and higher education. Along the way, he has led professional organizations and encouraged more kids to explore engineering.

Linda earned her degrees in Biological and Agricultural Engineering and built a career as an environmental engineer, technical writer, engineering educator in higher ed, and a published author. Having grown up in a rural community and been a first-generation college student, she understands the power of connecting all students to STEM opportunities, regardless of zip code or skin color.

Together, Claude and Linda Hargrove founded STEM Dreams, LLC to help families and educators inspire the next generation of STEM Dreamers. This workbook is one way they hope to share that spark.

Bin 1:
Paper-based Activities

Paper Cup Helicopter

MATERIALS
- Paper cup
- Scissors
- Pen, pencil or marker

STEPS
1. Mark the bottom and sides of the cup as shown in the diagram. The lines stop about 3/4 in (2cm) from the bottom)
2. Cut along the lines so that you have 8 strips or "fins".
3. Fold every other fin at an angle. Make it roughly the same angle for each of the folded fins. You're done.
4. Hold your helicopter so that the bottom is parallel with the floor, release it, and watch it twirl to the floor. The tips of fins can be facing up or down, if you like.
   NOTE: There's no need to twist you hand while releasing.

EXPERIMENT
To show adaptability, try dropping the helicopter sideways. What do you need to change in your design to make it perform the way you want? Use critical thinking to analyze the problem and form a new hypothesis.

WHAT MAKES IT WORK

The STEM concepts at play here are aerodynamics and physics. The helicopter twirls because of the way air flows around the fins. It falls because of the combination of the pull of gravity and the drag from the weight of the materials you used to make your simple twirling craft.

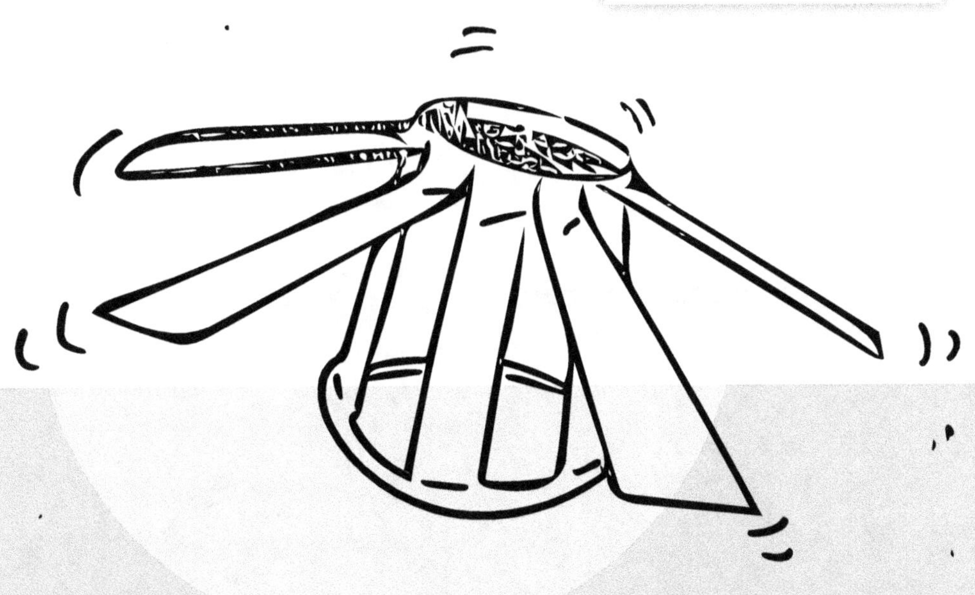

RE-IMAGINE IT!

What was the hardest part, and what was your plan for figuring it out?

Draw your idea here:

BUILT FROM CURIOSITY

URSULA BURNS

Ursula Burns (born in 1958) was the first black woman to be a CEO (the boss) of a major corporation in the United States. This means she was the boss of Xerox Company from 2009 to 2016.

Growing up in Manhattan's Baruch Houses public housing, Ursula excelled at math from an early age, despite limited opportunities. Her mother's mantra "where you are is not who you are" shaped Ursula's ambition.

As she went through school, she developed her curiousity about STEM but also about leadership. She is known for self-belief and hard work that leads to transformation.

In 2021, she wrote a book using her mother's inspirational motto as the title. She credits all her success to her mother's influence.

Ursula's success came from self-belief and hard work, demonstrating incredible personal responsibility.

DREAM B.G.

Seed Paper

MATERIALS

* Used printer or notebook paper
* Bowl filled with water (large enough to hold your paper shreds)
* Cloth towel and/or paper towels
* Seeds (zinnia or marigold seeds work great)
* Waterproof flat surface like a cutting board
* Rolling pin or a tall drinking glass

STEPS

* Tear or cut the paper into pieces, the smaller the better.
* Place the paper shreds into the bowl and fill at least halfway with water
* Let the shreds soak overnight. The paper should be really soggy the next day.
* Scoop all the wet paper out and wad it into a ball, squeezing as much water out as possible.
* Gently mix into the seeds (be careful not to break the seed apart).
* Using the rolling pin (or drinking glass), roll the seeded paper pulp into a thin layer on the cutting board. Sop any excess water with cloth or paper towels. Allow the seed paper to fully dry.
* Cut the seed paper into small squares. Plant the squares under a thin layer of soil. Water it well. The seeds should germinate (sprout) in a few days.

EXPERIMENT
Try different colors of paper and different seeds. Grow the seeds in sand instead of soil.

WHAT MAKES IT WORK
Paper is made from wood pulp. Pulp is at play here. The process of making paper from chewed up wood (pine trees, mostly) uses a lot of water. When we re-wet paper, the fibers break down into pulp again.

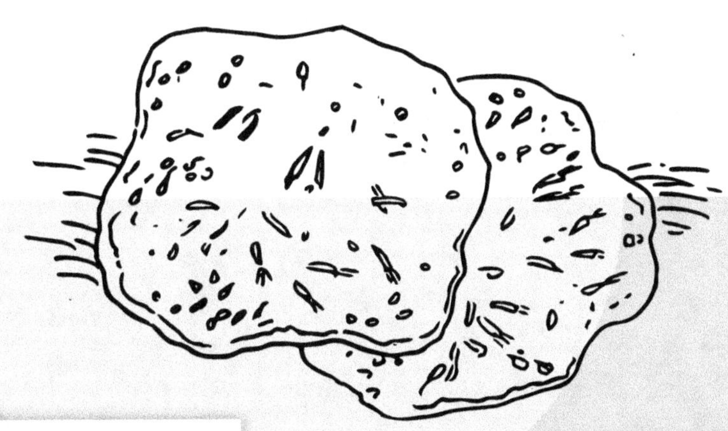

Happy planting!

RE-IMAGINE IT!

What was the hardest part, and what was your plan for figuring it out?

Draw your idea here:

BUILT FROM CURIOSITY

ELIJAH J. MCCOY

Elijah McCoy was born in Canada in 1844. He grew up in Michigan (USA) where he loved tinkering with tools and taking things apart just to see how they worked.

His curiosity for machines started when he was very young. He was always fixing, building, and experimenting. At just 15 years old, Elijah traveled all the way to Scotland to study mechanical engineering, a big achievement for an African American at that time.

Later, he invented a special lubricating device that kept train engines running smoothly without stopping. His clever invention changed travel and industry and earned him more than 50 patents!

People admired his work so much they asked for "the real McCoy," meaning the best quality. Elijah's creativity and determination show that great ideas can come from anyone with curiosity and persistence.

Facing racial bias that limited his job options, Elijah showed adaptability by focusing on creating his own work and inventing.

DREAM BIG.

String Spinner

MATERIALS

- Thick paper or light cardboard (used cereal boxes or old greeting cards are good)
- Thin paper (for tracing the template on the next page)
- Spring, yarn, or twine (24 in/60cm)
- Scissors
- Ruler
- Pencil or pen to trace and make holes in the paper
- Colorful markers (optional)

STEPS

- **Cut the cirle:** Use the ruler to create a 5in (12cm) circle on the thick paper. The semicircle on the next page can be used as a guide. Cut it out carefully.
- **Make the holes:** Use the pencil or pen to make two small holes near the center about 1/4 in (1cm) apart
- **Add the string:** Pull the ends of the string through both holes and tie the ends together to make a loop.
- **Make it spin:** Slide the circle along the string so that you have the same amount of string on both sides of the circle. Hold one end of the loop in each hand and swing the spinner until the string twists (20-30 twists). Stop spinning and gently pull your hands apart. The spinner should spin fast. Next relax your hands to let the string twist back the other way.

EXPERIMENT

What happens when your circle is twice as large or half as small? Does a different kind of string make the spinner go faster or slower?

WHAT MAKES IT WORK

Something called **angular momentum** is at play here. When you twist up the string, you're building up energy like in a spring. Pulling on the string, converts that energy into motion. Friction in the string, slows the spinner down.

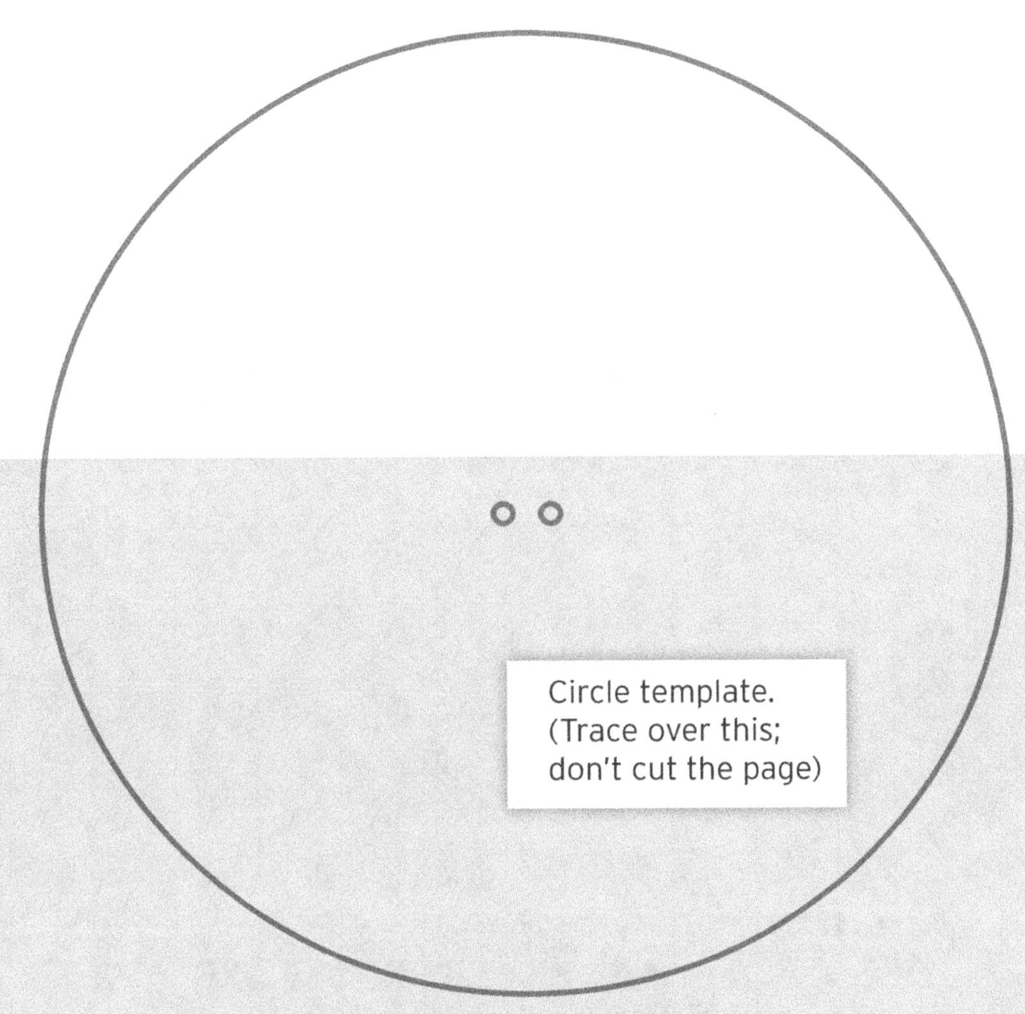

RE-IMAGINE IT!

What was the hardest part, and what was your plan for figuring it out?

Draw your idea here:

BUILT FROM CURIOSITY

ANTONIA NOVELLO

Born in 1944, Dr. Antonia Novello is a Puerto Rican physician and public health leader who made history as the first woman and the first Hispanic person to serve as Surgeon General of the United States.

As a child, Antonia faced serious health challenges, which inspired her to pursue a career in medicine and dedicate her life to helping others. With the support of her mother, a school principal who personally tutored her, Antonia completed high school at just 15 years old.

Throughout her career, Dr. Novello worked tirelessly to improve healthcare for children, women, and underserved communities.

Antonia Novello's life and work demonstrate how compassion, determination, and courage can create lasting change and inspire future generations. She took personal responsiblity for addressing major public health issues like tobacco use, AIDS, and children's health.

DREAM BIG.

Straw Rocket

MATERIALS

* 2 sheets of printer paper (A4 size, 8.5" x 11")
* 1 Number 2 pencil
* Drinking straw
* Tape
* Scissors
* Markers for decoration (optional)

STEPS

* Roll the rectangle the long way with the fold line on the top. You can roll it around a pencil to get it tight. Tape it along the sides to secure it.
* Fold it over at the top on the part that says fold. Secure the fold with tape to keep it down.
* Cut two 2" squares of paper in half to make right triangles. Tape them to the open end of the paper tube to make 'fins', equally spaced around the end.
* Slide a drinking straw into the open end and blow hard. Watch your rocket take flight.

EXPERIMENT

* Try to make the rocket with a paper that's thinner, like tracing paper. How does it affect how high the rocket goes? Do you expect it to go higher or will there be no change at all?
* Instead of blowing air through the straw, can you think of other ways to use a stream of air to make the rocket go up? What happens when you make the pointy end (the nose of the rocket) pointier?

WHAT MAKES IT WORK

So gravity is at play here in a big way, as well as air pressure. Air is your rocket fuel for this paper aircraft. When you think like a rocket scientist you try to get more lift by using the same amount or less fuel.

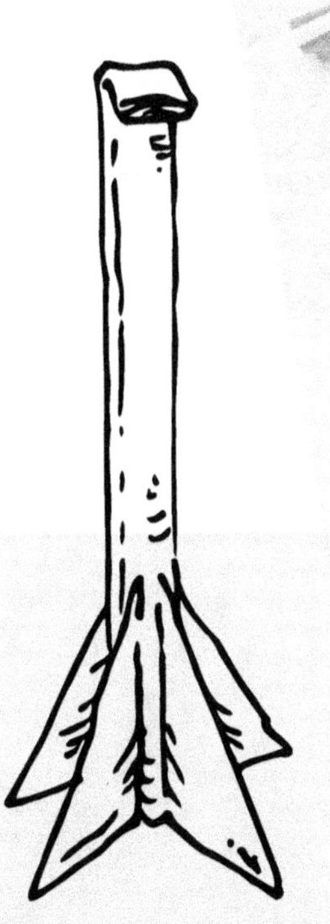

Up, up, and away!

RE-IMAGINE IT!

What was the hardest part, and what was your plan for figuring it out?

Draw your idea here:

BUILT FROM CURIOSITY

MAE JEMISON

Dr. Mae C. Jemison always dreamed of exploring the stars. She was born in Alabama in 1956. In 1992, she became the first African-American woman to go to space aboard the Space Shuttle Endeavour.

As a child, she loved science, dancing, and imagining herself flying into space. She studied hard, becoming a medical doctor and a chemical engineer before joining NASA. The TV show *Star Trek* inspired her dreams of star travel when she was young. A year after her groundbreaking space flight, she appeared as actor on the show.

Mae is also a business owner and researcher. She has founded a research company, an educational foundation, and contributed to the 100 Year Starship project. She's been inducted into the National Women's Hall of Fame.

She showed empathy by serving as a medical volunteer in West Africa and later by dedicating her post-NASA career to improving science literacy globally.

DREAM BIG.

Paper Cup Telephone

MATERIALS

- 2 Paper cups
- 2 Toothpicks
- Yarn or string (at least 10 feet or 3 meters)
- Scissors
- Ruler or tape measure

STEPS

- **Create the holes:** Use the pointed tip of a toothpick or a pencil to carefully poke a small hole in the center of the bottom of each cup. Try to keep the hole as small as possible to prevent the string from slipping out.
- **Thread the string:** Insert one end of the string through the hole in one of the cups from the outside in. Repeat this step for the other cup.
- **Secure the string:** Tie the end of the string around a toothpick inside each cup, making sure the knot is large enough to prevent the string from pulling back through the hole. If needed, break the toothpick slightly so it fits inside the cup but remains long enough to keep the string in place.
- **Set up your telephone:** Hold one cup while a friend holds the other. Walk apart until the string is stretched tight between you.
- **Test your telephone:** One person should place the open end of their cup firmly around their mouth and speak softly. The other person should hold the open end of their cup against their ear and listen.

EXPERIMENT

Does the telephone work the same if you don't keep the string tight? Try a thicker or thinner string. Try a thin plastic or Nylon cord. Does a man-made material work better than natural fibers like cotton, jute, and wood?

WHAT MAKES IT WORK

Sound waves are at play here. Sound travels through the air and creates vibrations that travel along the string in mechanical waves (longitudinal waves) and to your ear. A real telephone uses the same process, except instead of physical waves traveling along the wires, it uses electrical signals.

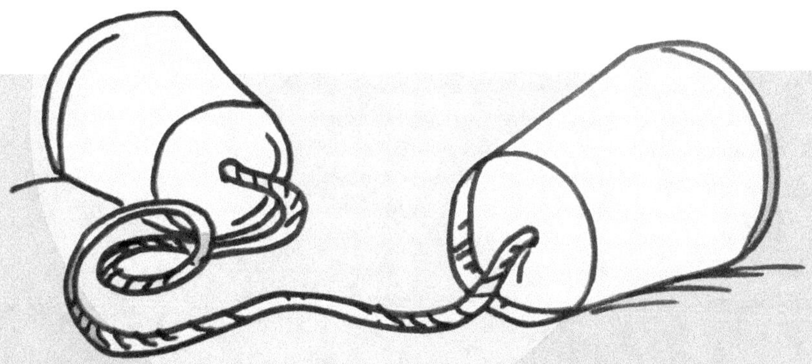

Team up. Use your communication skills to decide on a design.

RE-IMAGINE IT!

What was the hardest part, and what was your plan for figuring it out?

Draw your idea here:

BUILT FROM CURIOSITY

GRANVILLE WOODS

Granville T. Woods was born in 1856 in Ohio. He was an self-taught electrical and mechanical engineer whose inventions improved transportation and communication across the USA. As a boy, he was an apprentice in a machine shop and learning about machines and metals.

Often called "The Black Edison," he earned more than 50 patents, including the multiplex telegraph which was a system allowing train stations to communicate with moving trains. His work made railways safer and made them work better. Woods also developed electrical devices used in trolleys and amusement parks.

Sometimes, he didn't get credit for his work because of his race. He spoke up for himself and he was persistent. His achievements remind us that curiosity and determination can create technologies that change how the world moves and communicates.

Granville had to be incredibly adaptable, inventing solutions across various fields, including telegraphy, telephones, and electric railways.

DREAM BIG.

Paper Airplane

MATERIALS
Square of paper, approximately 4 in^2 (10cm^2)
Markers for decorating (optional)

STEPS
These instructions are for a classic folded plane called the
Bulldog Dart.

- Create a center crease:
  Fold your paper in half lengthwise, then unfold it. This
  crease will be your guideline for the next steps.
- Fold the top corners:
  Bring the top two corners down so they meet along the
  center crease.
- Fold the corners again:
  Flip the paper over, then fold the new top corners in
  toward the center crease once more. The diagonal
  edges should line up evenly with the middle.
- Form the nose:
  Fold the top point down so the tip meets the bottom of
  where the previous folds come together. This creates
  the Bulldog's short, blunt "snub" nose.
- Fold in half:
  Fold the entire plane in half along the original center
  crease, with the folds on the inside.
- Make the wings:
  Fold each wing down so the top edge lines up with the
  bottom of the nose. Repeat on the other side to match.

EXPERIMENT

Try thin paper or thicker paper. Does it still work the same? How about a rectangular sheet of paper?

WHAT MAKES IT WORK

Aerodynamics is at play here, once again. Because we're working with the gravitational pull against a sheet of paper, it comes down to the amount of thrust and angle of launch to create the perfect flight.

NOTE: softer throws get better results. Why do you think so? Use the next page to improve on this design.

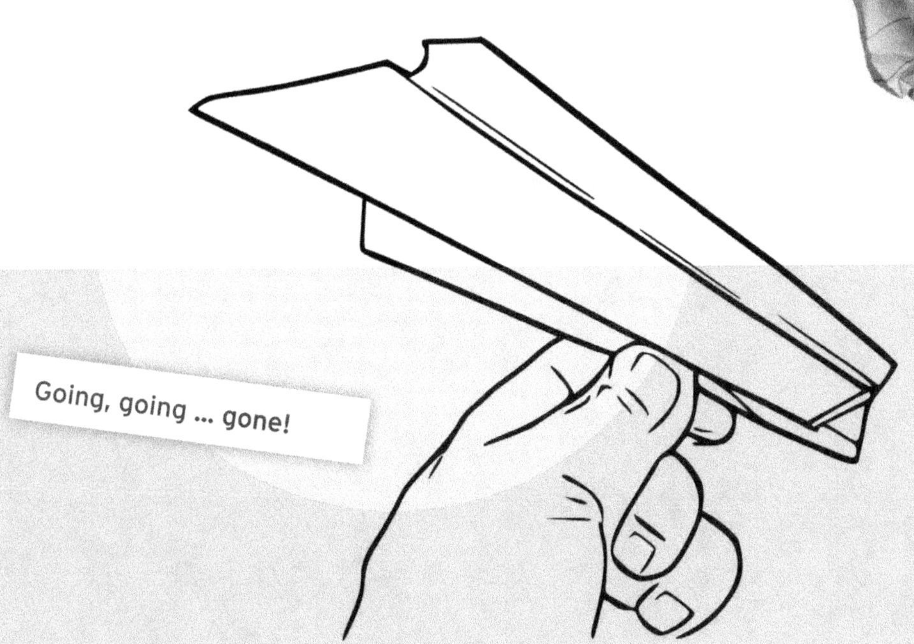

RE-IMAGINE IT!

What was the hardest part, and what was your plan for figuring it out?

Draw your idea here:

BUILT FROM CURIOSITY

GRACE HOPPER

Born in New York City in 1906, Grace Hopper's hands-on nature surfaced dramatically around age seven when she decided to figure out how an alarm clock worked. She was so determined that she dismantled seven of them before her mother intervened and limited her to just one.

She was raised in a household that strongly valued education. Her father believed in equal educational opportunity, and her mother had studied geometry, creating a supportive intellectual environment. She went on to attend Vassar College and later Yale University.

In 1944, Grace joined the U.S. Navy, marking the start of her groundbreaking career in computer science. She became one of the pioneers in the field. Among her achievements was the creation of COBOL, a computer programming language.

Before the end of her military career, Grace Hopper had achieved the distinct honor of U.S. Navy Rear Admiral. She was a champion of clear communication.

DREAM BIG.

Walking Paper Horse

MATERIALS

- Paper (cardstock works best)
- Scissors
- Ruler
- Pencil
- Large flat rigid surface (book, for instance)

STEPS

- Draw the lines as shown
- Cut the cardstock as shown
- Bend the four 'legs' down at a 90 degree angle
- Turn the horse over and bend the tail and head up, curling the tail with the edge of the scissors. Crimp the head, as shown
- Snip the corners of the legs as shown
- Place the horse (legs down) on a large flat surface (a closed book or shoe box lid)
- Tilt the surface and watch the horse trot

EXPERIMENT

Tilt the surface more and see what happens to the horse's gait. Is there an angle at which the horse falls? Is there an angle at which the horse doesn't move at all? Will this horse work with thinner paper?

WHAT MAKES IT WORK

The forces of gravity and friction are at play here. Gravity pulls the horse down the inclined plane (tilted flat surface) but it has to overcome the force of friction between the legs and the flat surface.

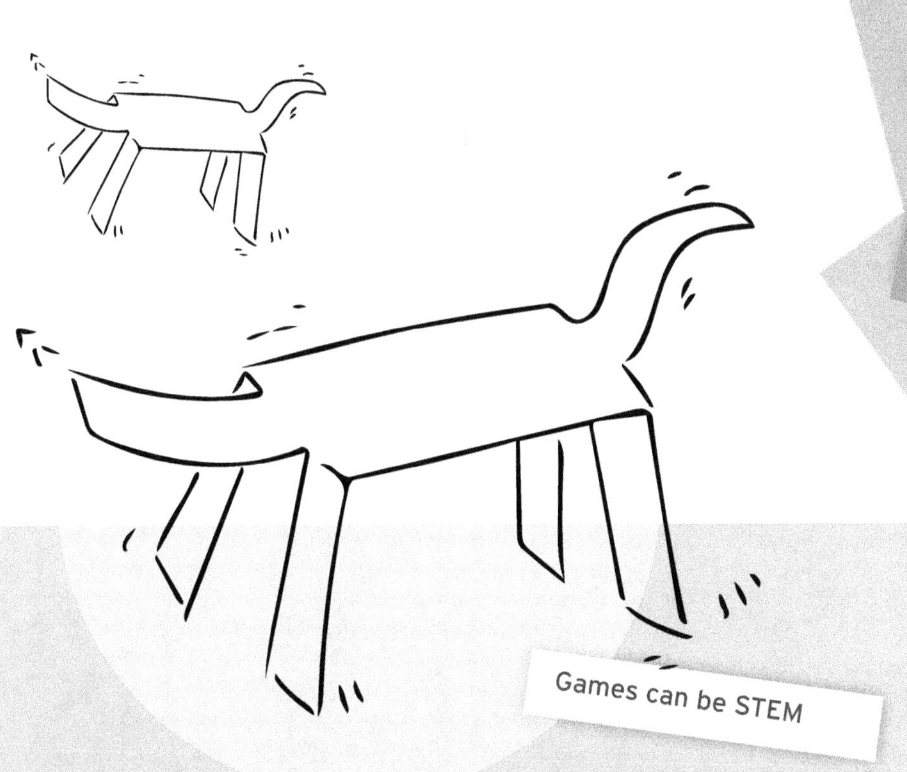

RE-IMAGINE IT!

What was the hardest part, and what was your plan for figuring it out?

Draw your idea here:

BUILT FROM CURIOSITY

DAVID H. BLACKWELL

Born in a small Illinois town in 1919, David Harold Blackwell excelled at geometry and statistics (two branches of mathematics) in high school. As a young boy though, he didn't really like math but he was good at it. His excellence in his studies allowed him to be promoted quickly through school. He ended up getting all three of his degrees by the age of 22, despite the extreme racial discrimination at the time.

He went on to study game theory, probability theory, and statistics. These are topics which formed the foundation of modern data science and artificial intelligence (AI) which we use everyday in work and play.

David used profound critical thinking to develop new mathematical models and theorems still used in decision-making today.

In 2024, the computer company NVIDIA developed a highly specialized computer chip and named it after Dr. Blackwell. It's called the Blackwell Graphics Processing Unit (GPU).

DREAM BIG.

Paper Tube Parachute

MATERIALS

- Paper cup or empty toilet paper tube
- Pen or pencil (sharpened)
- Scissors
- String or yarn (at least 12 inches)
- Plastic grocery sack/bag (with no rips or holes) with handles

STEPS

- Using the pen or sharpened pencil, carefully poke holes at two places, as shown, near the top of the cup or paper tube. This is your parachute 'basket'
- Cut the string in half and tie one piece of string in each of the two holes in the parachute basket
- Tie the other end of the string to the handles of the plastic sack
- You're ready to fly

EXPERIMENT

Use a different size bag. How does that change the parachute's flight? Use a different size basket. What are your results? How does placing a small toy in the basket affect the flight of the parachute? Vary the size of the parachute.

WHAT MAKES IT WORK

Gravity and air resistance are at play here. Balancing the forces keeps the parachute floating longer. The resistance provided by the bag slows the rate at which the parachute falls. If the basket (and its contents) outweigh the air resistance provided by the plastic bag, the parachute falls quicker.

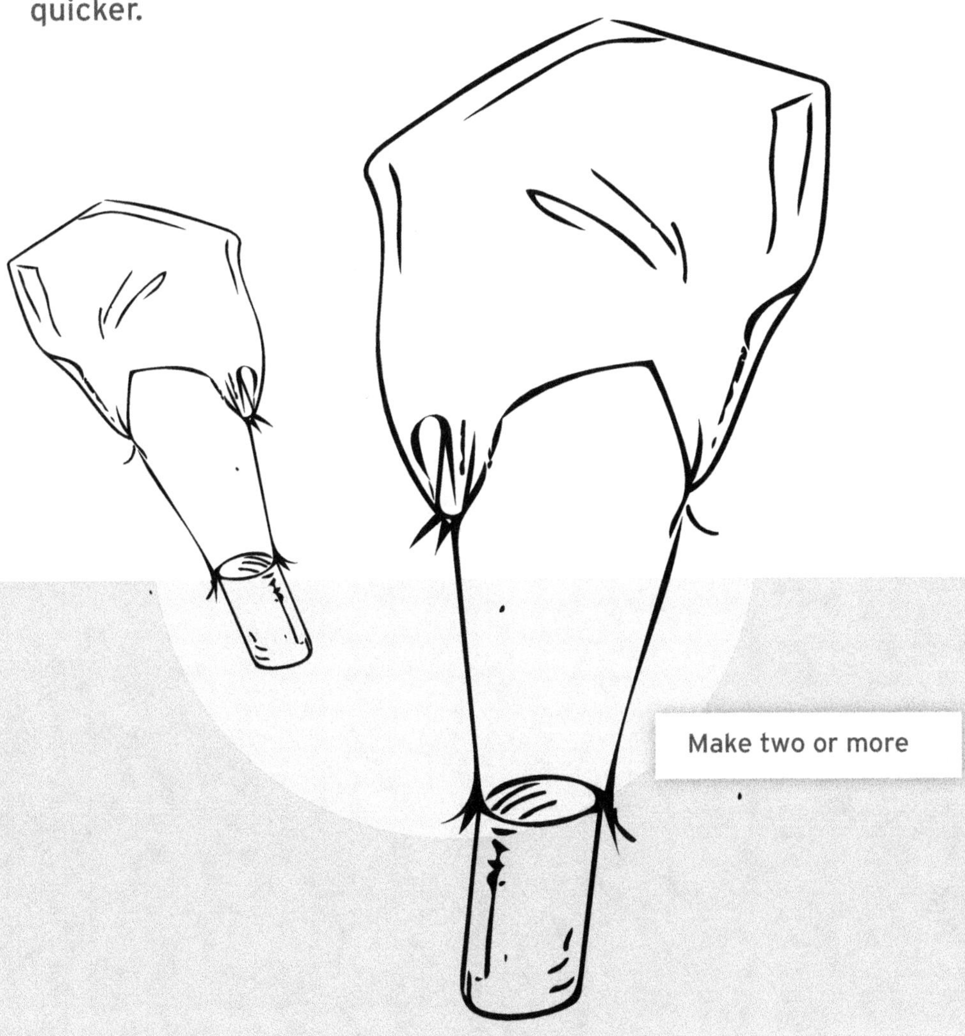

RE-IMAGINE IT!

What was the hardest part, and what was your plan for figuring it out?

Draw your idea here:

BUILT FROM CURIOSITY

WINSTON E. SCOTT

Winston E. Scott was born in Florida in 1950. He loved two things as a boy, building things and playing music! He was curious about how things worked, which made him go on to study engineering. He also became a talented trumpet player.

Winston didn't stop there! He flew airplanes for the United States Navy and even earned a master's degree in Aeronautical Engineering. Later, he became a NASA astronaut and flew on the Space Shuttle Endeavour and Columbia. He even walked in space! Winston showed that you can be good at science and art. He's a real-life space musician and engineer!

Captain Scott wrote a book about his NASA space walks in 2005. It's called *Reflections from Earth Orbit*.

Winston Scott had to demonstrate extreme adaptability, quickly mastering new aircraft, complex space systems, and working in the zero-gravity environment.

DREAM B.G.

Bin 2:
Metal-based
Activities

Tin Can Screecher

MATERIALS

- Tin can (15 oz) (cleaned and dried out, with no sharp edges)
- Jute string or yarn (12 to 15 inches)
- Hammer
- Nail or screw
- Scissors
- Wet paper towel or rag

STEPS

- With a hammer and nail (or screw) punch a hole in the center of the tin can's lid.
- Cut a 12 to 15 inch length of jute string.
- From the inside of the can, thread one end of the string through the hole.
- Tie a knot at the end of the string so that the sting doesn't come out when pulled.
- Using a wet paper towel or rag, dampen the string.
- Grip the wet string from the inside of the can and pull down the length of the string, keeping steady pressure.
- You should hear a 'growling' noise come from inside the can.

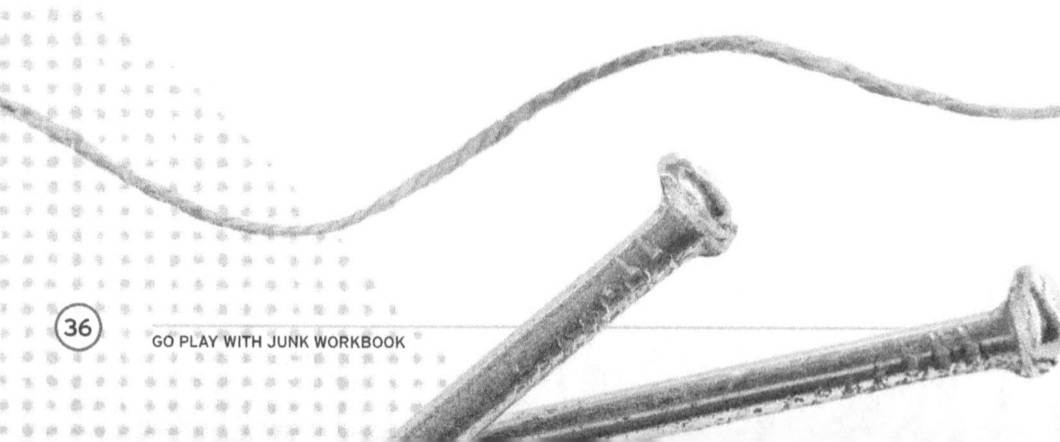

EXPERIMENT

Try using a shorter string. Then a longer string. A string of a different material. Does this change the sound that comes from the can?

WHAT MAKES IT WORK

The STEM concept at play here is the physics of vibration. Sound is created when energy is released as you create friction when you grip and pull the dampened string. This energy is sound and heat energy.

Things are about to get a little noisy.

RE-IMAGINE IT!

What part did you do all by yourself? What part did you need help with?

Draw your idea here:

BUILT FROM CURIOSITY

YVONNE Y. CLARK

Yvonne Young Clark was born in Houston, Texas, in 1929. When she was a little girl, she dreamed of becoming a pilot. She was very curious and loved to explore how things were made, and even how they came apart!

She was such a great student that she finished high school early, at just 16 years old. In 1951, she made history by becoming the first woman to earn a mechanical engineering degree from Howard University.

Even though there were many challenges for both Black people and women who wanted to work as engineers, Dr. Clark didn't give up. She kept learning and worked hard, eventually earning her PhD in engineering. She became an amazing teacher and leader in both schools and businesses. She was also a caring wife and mother. Dr. Clark passed away in 2019 at the age of 89.

Yvonne was a lifelong learner with a strong learner's mindset in the classroom and in industry.

DREAM BIG.

Votive Candle Holder

MATERIALS

* Tin cans (a few, 2.25 - 3.5oz); cleaned and dried with no sharp edges from removing one lid
* Magic marker
* Hammer
* Nail or screw; smaller are best
* Old towel or rag

STEPS

* Place the old towel or rag on a hard, flat surface (countertop, table, cutting board, etc.); doubling it up gives more cushion against impact and noise (you're about to be hammering a lot)
* Lay the can on the towel and use the marker to create a pattern of dots on the side of the can. Space the dots at least one half inch (about 1.25 cm) apart. Examples of patterns: heart shape, Christmas tree, smiley face
* With the hammer and nail, create a hole where you made a dot with the marker
* When you've finished your design, light your candle and enjoy the glow of the flame through your unique design

EXPERIMENT

Create multiple candle holders of the same size. They can all have the same design or variations on a theme. For instance, you can make candle holders and each has a different letter spelling the words JESUS, CHRISTMAS, or KWANZA.

WHAT MAKES IT WORK

The STEM concept at play here is light radiation. Candles give off three types of light radiation: visible light, infrared (IR) light, and thermal radiation. The flame burns hottest in the blue and white portions of the flame, closer to the wick, where the flame is consuming high amounts of oxygen. Burning candles give off water vapor and carbon dioxide, byproducts of combustion.

NOTE: If you are doing this project in a school or library setting, using a candle may not be allowed.

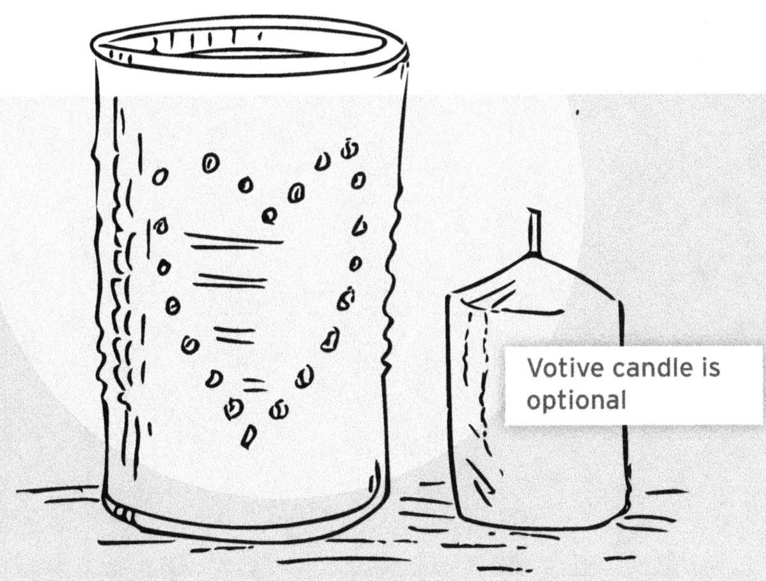

RE-IMAGINE IT!

What was the hardest part, and what was your
plan for figuring it out?

Draw your idea here:

BUILT FROM CURIOSITY

VALERIE L. THOMAS

Valerie L. Thomas was born in Maryland in 1943. At eight years old, her curiosity led her to check out *The Boy's First Book on Electronics* from the library. Her dad, who also liked to tinker, didn't help her with the projects. Back then, girls were often told science wasn't for them.

Valerie didn't let that stop her. She went on to study physics at Morgan State University and graduated in 1964. After college, she joined NASA as a mathematical data analyst, using her skills in math and science to solve complex problems.

At NASA, Valerie used her skills in collaboration to help with space research, created computer programs for satellite images, and invented the illusion transmitter, which inspired modern 3D movies and medical tools. She earned many honors, including the NASA Goddard Space Flight Center Award of Merit and the NASA Equal Opportunity Medal for her groundbreaking work and her efforts to make science more inclusive for everyone.

DREAM BIG.

Tin Can Stilts

MATERIALS

NOTE: because of the danger of sharp edges, we highly recommend parent supervision with this project

- 2 large aluminum cans, (about 46 oz, 1.36 L work great; they are about 7 inches tall)
- Several feet of rope or thick cord
- Two types of can openers: A lid remover and a punch opener to make a triangular opening
- Duct tape

STEPS

- Make sure the cans are emptied, cleaned and dried and of the same size.
- Safely remove the top of the can and discard it. Put duct tape over the sharp edges of the can's opening.
- Using the can punch opener, make two holes, opposite each other, about 1 inch from the bottom.
- MAKE THE ROPE HANDLES: Thread the end of the rope through one hole, inside the can, and through the opposite hole. Pull the rope through until one end is slightly above the waist of the person standing on the bottom of the can. Then, with sides of the rope held taut, cut the longer end. With both ends about waist-high, tie the ends. Repeat this for the other can.
- Have fun walking tall!

EXPERIMENT

Test your balance by using smaller cans to create stilts. Walk on different surfaces and compare how easy or difficult it is to walk across sand, grass, concrete, or rocky ground using your stilts.

WHAT MAKES IT WORK

These tin-can stilts are fun to develop balance skills but there are other things at play here. You're exploring the physical properties like your center of gravity as you shift (distribute) your body weight in order to stay balanced over the cans. distribution and balance. You're also testing the material science and mechanical engineering of the humble can. Most 'tin' cans are made of aluminum or steel. These metals have great stress-to-weight properties that prevent them from crumpling under the stress of your weight. Ever wonder why most cans are cylinders? Simple. Their circular shape evenly distributes weight which makes it better for bearing weight (and for making stilts).

Slow and steady!

RE-IMAGINE IT!

What was the hardest part, and what was your plan for figuring it out?

Draw your idea here:

BUILT FROM CURIOSITY

EMMETT W. CHAPPELLE

Emmett Chappelle was born in Phoenix, Arizona, in 1925. As a child, he attended an all-Black one-room schoolhouse. After finishing high school in 1942, he was drafted into the U.S. Army and served in Italy during World War II.

When the war ended, Emmett went to college and earned degrees in electrical engineering and biology. He became a biochemistry professor and did groundbreaking research in biomedical science, astrobiology, remote sensing, and genetics. From 1966 to 2001, he worked at NASA, where he studied how things glow, a process called fluorescence and bioluminescence. Dr. Chappelle held 14 patents and was inducted into the National Inventors Hall of Fame.

Dr. Chappelle passed away in 2019 at the age of 93, but his discoveries and adaptability continue to inspire scientists today. His research showed how to detect living cells in soil and how to find cancer cells in mice, work that remains important to NASA and researchers around the world.

DREAM BIG.

Magic Rolling Can

MATERIALS

- Empty metal soft drink can (no dents or deformities)
- Latex balloon (12 inch works best)
- PVC pipe (12 to 18 inches), optional

STEPS

- **CHARGE THE BALLOON:** Rub the balloon against your hair, a wool sweater, or piece of fuzzy fabric (fake fur works wonders). A half a dozen swipes should be enough to 'charge' the balloon.

- **MOVING THE CAN:** Place the soda can on its side on a flat surface (kitchen countertop, for example). Make sure nothing is in the way that will stop it from rolling. Slowly bring the 'charged' balloon close to the can. The can should roll toward the balloon.

EXPERIMENT

Try a short section of PVC pipe instead of a balloon. Does it work better, worse, or about the same? How about a piece of fake fur? What other objects could you use to "charge up" to move the can? Will a wooden spoon work? How about another empty metal can? Can you move two cans back to back?

WHAT MAKES IT WORK

Electrostatics is at play here. As you rub the balloon or pipe over your hair, you are stripping electrons from your hair to the balloon. Electrons are negatively charged and they build up on the balloon (or pipe).

There's an excess of negative charges and they want to go somewhere. When you bring it close to something like a can or a wall, it sticks because the positive charges in that object 'stick' to the negative charges in the balloon.

Opposites attract!

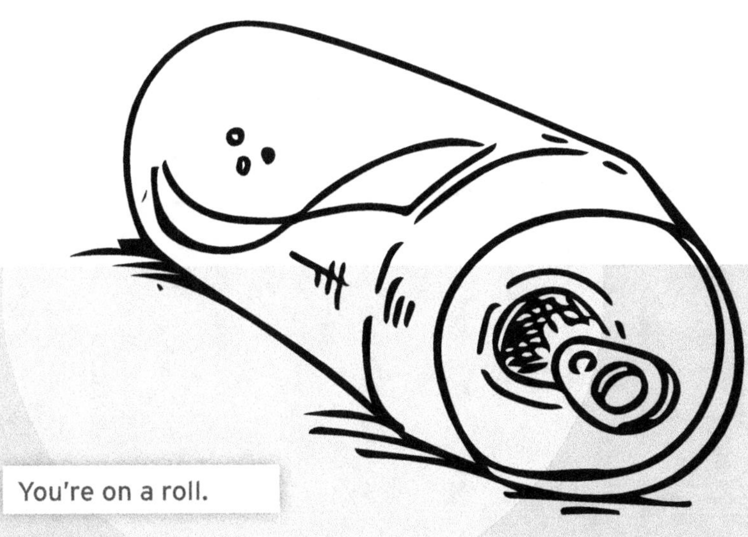

You're on a roll.

RE-IMAGINE IT!

What was the hardest part, and what was your plan for figuring it out?

Draw your idea here:

BUILT FROM CURIOSITY

HERTHA AYRTON

Hertha Ayrton was a British scientist, engineer, and inventor born in 1854. She loved learning and solving problems. It wasn not common for women to study science when she was a young girl.

She didn't let that stop her. Hertha invented a special tool to draw perfect lines for math and engineering, called the line divider. She also studied electricity and discovered why electric lights sometimes flicker, which was an important discovery that made streetlights safer and more reliable.

Later, during World War I, she invented a fan to clear dangerous gas from trenches and save soldiers' lives. Hertha was one of the first women to be recognized by the Royal Society of London for her work in science. She believed strongly in equality and often spoke up for women's rights. Hertha Ayrton's curiosity, creativity, and courage are inspirational.

Hertha used critical thinking skills to solve problems in mathematics and electrical engineering.

DREAM B.G.

Bin 3: Plastics-based Activities

Self-Starting Siphon

MATERIALS

- 2 cups or glasses of equal size (10 oz or about 295 mL is good)
- 3 plastic bendy straws (you can try paper straws but plastic works best because of the water)
- Scissors
- Masking tape
- A box equal to the height of the cup
- Access to water

STEPS

- Prepare the three straws like so:
    1. Straw 1: Trim away the longer portion so that you have about the same amount of straw on either side of the bend.
    2. Straw 2: Make two cuts, leaving about 1 in (2.5cm) on either side of the bendy part
    3. Straw 3: Do not cut
- Connect the segments with tape so that they form an M shape with one "leg" being shorter than the other
- Place one cup on the box and the other cup on the table to one side of the box
- Fill the cup on the box to the brim
- Hold the siphon like an M, as shown, above the water in the cup. The upper humps of the M should be about level. Then insert the siphon into the water quickly, maintaining the M shape. A stream of water should start flowing from the longer exposed arm of the M. If it does not, remove it, shake out the excess water, and try inserting it again.

EXPERIMENT

What happens when you insert the siphon slowly? Why is it important to insert it in the M shape? Try changing the proportions of the M shape. Does the siphon still work?

What Makes it Work:
This activity demonstrates the principles of siphoning, a process that moves liquid from a higher container to a lower one using atmospheric pressure and gravity.

When you insert the M-shaped straw siphon into the water correctly, liquid starts moving through the straw and flows into the lower cup. This happens because gravity pulls the water down through the longer side of the straw.

Something called cohesion (water sticking to itself) helps pull more water along, keeping the flow going.

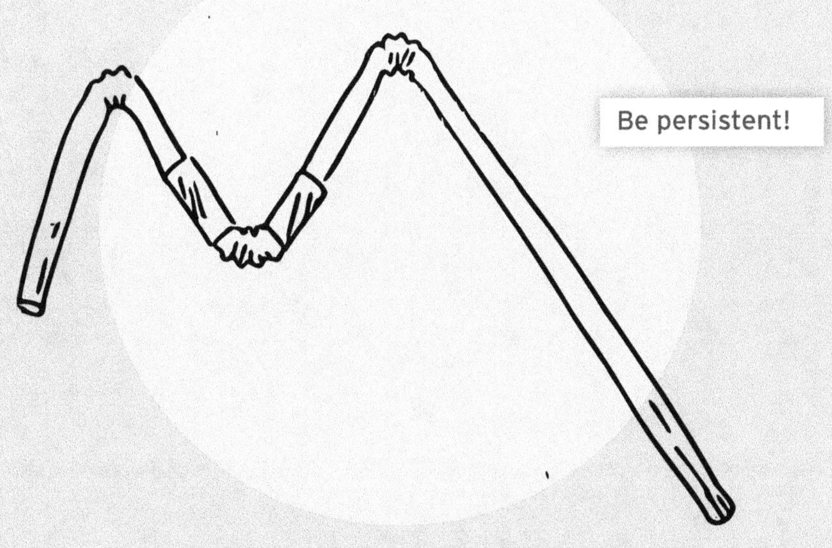

RE-IMAGINE IT!

What was the hardest part, and what was your plan for figuring it out?

Draw your idea here:

BUILT FROM CURIOSITY

GARRETT MORGAN

Garrett Morgan was an inventive problem-solver who made everyday life safer. He was born in Kentucky in 1877 and went on to become a self-taught engineer and entrepreneur who invented the modern traffic signal and an early version of the gas mask, saving countless lives.

Safety was important to Garrett. He's also known for a safety hood that was used by firefighters and rescue workers. His inventions helped to cut down on accidents. Because of his concern for his community, he also founded a newspaper to empower everyone with information.

Garrett was inducted into the National Inventors Hall of Fame. He showed that engineers can use creativity to solve real-world problems that protect people. His story shows us that innovation starts with noticing a problem and having the courage to fix it, no matter who you are or where you start.

Garrett's empathy was the foundation of his work. He saw dangerous problems and invented ways to protect and save people.

DREAM B.G.

Bubble Bundle Wand

MATERIALS

- Plastic drinking straws (3-5)
- Scissors
- Hot glue gun
- Hot glue sticks
- Bubble solution (store-bought is fine)
- Dinner plate or shallow bowl

STEPS

Cut each drinking straw in thirds (about 2.75 inches or 7cm)
Using the hot glue gun, glue the short straw sections together to form a bundle
Pour bubble solution into a shallow bowl or dinner plate
Let the bubble bundle drain slightly before blowing bubbles

EXPERIMENT

Add more straw sections to the bundle. Is there a limit to how big your bundle can be?
Try different bubble solutions or make your own. Keep reading the What Makes it Work section for tips and tricks for longer-lasting bubble experiments.

WHAT MAKES IT WORK

Surface tension is at play here. If you make your own bubbles, it helps to use glycerin (food safe is preferable) and table sugar to extend the surface tension. The right amount of surface tension in your bubble solution creates bubbles that last while they float like diamonds in the air.

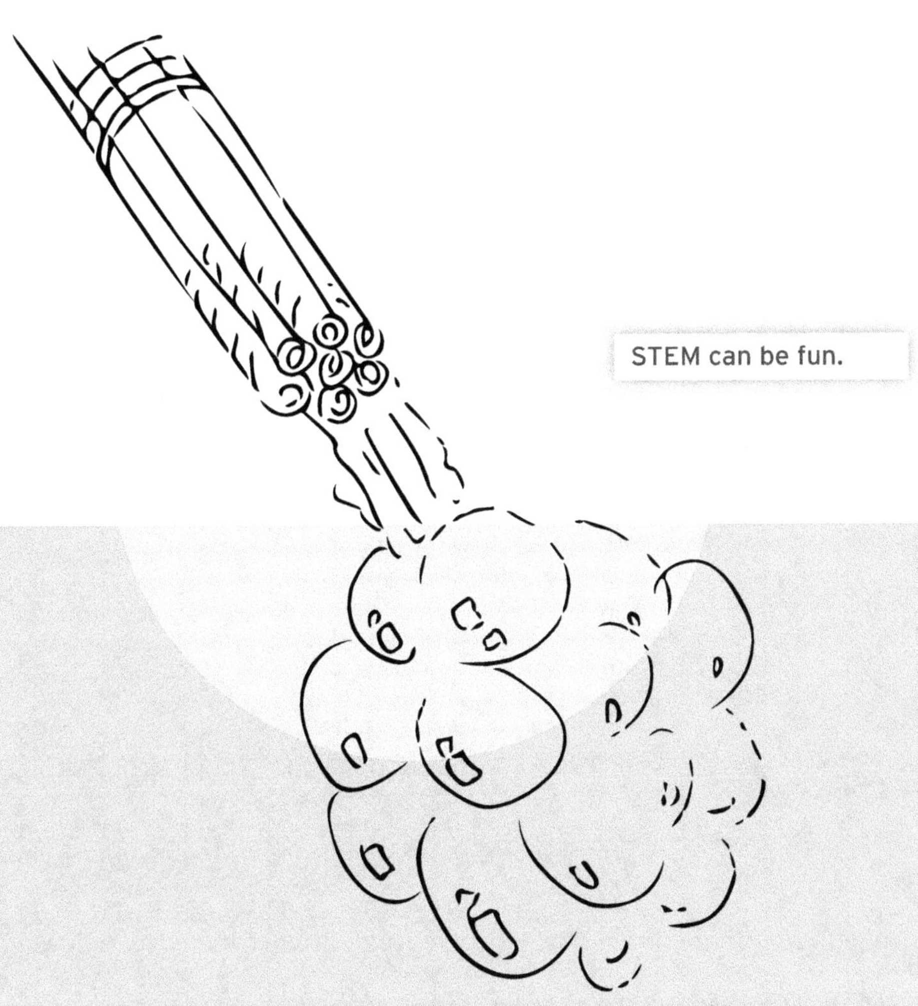

RE-IMAGINE IT!

What was the hardest part, and what was your plan for figuring it out?

Draw your idea here:

BUILT FROM CURIOSITY

APRILLE ERICSSON-JACKSON

Dr. Aprille Ericsson-Jackson is an award-winning mechanical and aerospace engineer at NASA, and the first Black woman to earn a Ph.D. in mechanical engineering from Howard University. Born in 1963 in Brooklyn, New York, Aprille remembers watching the Apollo space missions when she was around six years old. This is when her interest in astronauts started.

At NASA's Goddard Space Flight Center, she's worked on satellite and spacecraft missions that explore our planet and the universe beyond. Dr. Ericsson-Jackson is also a passionate advocate for diversity in STEM, mentoring young scientists and encouraging girls to pursue engineering.

Her journey from a curious child who loved math and science to a leader in aerospace shows that persistence, confidence, and creativity can open doors to the stars.

Aprille used critical thinking skills to solve complex problems of satellite orbit and fluid dynamics in space missions.

DREAM BIG.

Plastic Fabric

MATERIALS

* 1 to 3 thin plastic grocery bags/sacks
* Scissors
* Clothing iron
* Heavy cardboard (large piece to cover work surface)
* Large paper bag or parchment paper (same size as the sheet of cardboard)

Adult supervision is strongly recommended for children under 12 years old.

STEPS

Preparing the bags: Trim the grocery bags as shown. Smooth the bag flat and fold over as indicated in the drawing until you have 8 layers of plastic.

Warming the iron: Turn your iron on to the Rayon Setting and allow it to heat up. If this is a steam iron, make sure there is no water in it.

Protecting the surfaces: Place the heavy cardboard flat on your work surface. This could be a table, an ironing board, or a kitchen countertop. The cardboard will protect the work surface from damage from heat or melted plastic bags. Place the folded plastic in the center of the cardboard and cover with parchment paper so that no plastic will be exposed directly to the iron. Never iron directly on the plastic. It will stick to the iron. And don't do this project on a glass surface. That's dangerous. The glass could break.

Ironing the plastic: Press the plastic for 30 to 40 seconds, keeping the iron in constant motion. Carefully lift the parchment paper (it will be very warm) and check on the plastic. If the edges have been melted together, you're done. If not, repeat the ironing process for about 20 more seconds.

EXPERIMENT
Try making something useful out of your plastic 'fabric'. This picture shows a small pouch made with duct tape, buttons, and string. What other things can you make? Here are some other plastics you can try in this way: plastic garbage bags and disposable plastic tablecloths.

WHAT MAKES IT WORK
Plastic fusion is at play here. Plastic shopping bags are known as thermoplastics. When heat is applied to thermoplastics, the polymers (or tiny plastic fibers) change their composition slightly and recombine. That's why you saw shrinkage after the plastic was ironed. Atmospheric pressure pushes on the water in the higher cup, helping to keep the flow continuous.

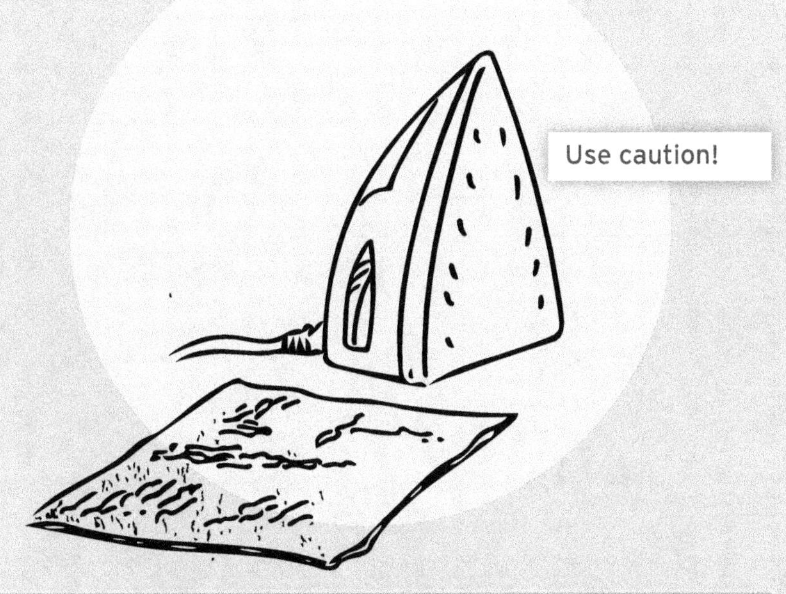

RE-IMAGINE IT!

What was the hardest part, and what was your plan for figuring it out?

Draw your idea here:

BUILT FROM CURIOSITY

AYANNA HOWARD

Dr. Ayanna Howard is a pioneering roboticist and engineer who blends creativity with cutting-edge technology. She began her career at NASA's Jet Propulsion Laboratory, where she developed intelligent robots designed for space exploration.

Today, she serves as the Dean of Engineering at The Ohio State University and is the founder of Zyrobotics, a company that creates educational robots and accessible technology for children with disabilities. Through her research in artificial intelligence and human-robot interaction, Dr. Howard is helping to make technology more inclusive and human-centered.

Born in 1972, Ayanna was fascinated by robots from a young age. Her favorite TV show, *The Bionic Woman*, inspired her belief that machines could be built to help people. Her journey shows that engineering isn't just about math and code. It's also about imagination, empathy, and the power to make a difference.

Ayanna's work demonstrates empathy, creating technology designed to assist and protect others.

DREAM B.G.

Watering Bottle

MATERIALS

- Empty plastic water bottle (~17 oz, 500mL)
- Small nail
- Hammer or pliers (optional)
- Access to water
- Plants in the garden that needs watering

STEPS

- **PREPARATION:** Make sure the empty water bottle is clean and dry.
- **MAKING THE HOLES:** Hold the empty water bottle upside down and make a series of holes in the bottom with the nail. The smaller the holes, the better. The holes should not be bigger than a pencil eraser. Five or six holes should be enough. Use a pair of pliers to grip the nail if it hurts your fingers
- **WATERING:** Take your waterer outside, fill it with water, and allow the water coming from the holes to water your garden.

EXPERIMENT

You may have noticed that the large holes make large streams of water that may be too much for smaller plants with tender leaves. How could you alter the design so that the waterer mimics a gentle rain? What happens when you cap the watering bottle after filling it with water?

Gravity and water surface tension are at play here. In fact, it is the pull of gravity through the holes that creates the water pressure.

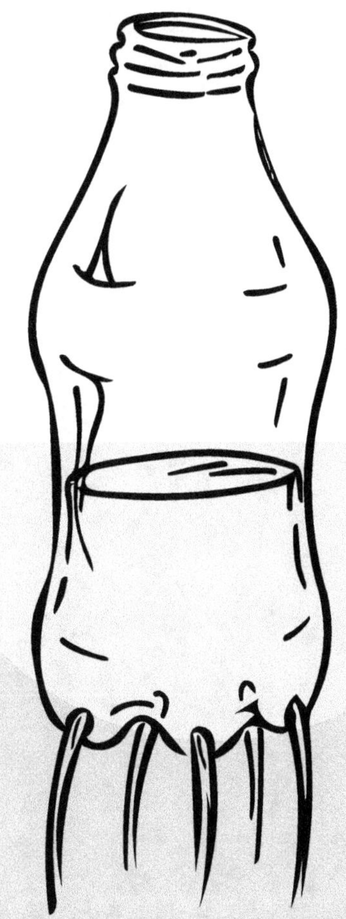

STEM can be practical

RE-IMAGINE IT!

What was the hardest part, and what was your plan for figuring it out?

Draw your idea here:

BUILT FROM CURIOSITY

LISA P. JACKSON

Lisa P. Jackson was born in 1962. In 2009, she made history as the first Black woman to lead the U.S. Environmental Protection Agency (EPA). EPA is the main team that works to keep the air, water, and soil in the United States clean and healthy.

Before leading the EPA, Lisa studied chemical engineering and spent 16 years working for the agency. Growing up in New Orleans, Louisiana, she didn't even like "outdoorsy" things much. But after college, she decided she wanted to help the environment, so she spent time cleaning up polluted areas.

As the director of the U.S. EPA, Lisa took personal responsibility for environmental protection and public health, often tackling large, complex issues like climate change and pollution control.

Now, Lisa works for Apple Inc., making sure their products and business are good for the environment. Her passion inspires all of us to work hard for a cleaner, better tomorrow.

DREAM BIG.

Hot & Cold Bottle

MATERIALS

- Empty water bottle
- Latex balloon
- Two bowls
- Access to water
- Ice
- Towel for water spills

STEPS

- Fit the balloon, uninflated, over the opening of the empty (and dry) water bottle
- Fill one bowl halfway with ice water
- Fill the other bowl halfway with piping hot water (be careful)
- Place the bottle, bottom first, into the bowl of hot water and observe what happens to the balloon
- Next, place the bottle, bottom first, into the bowl of ice water. Observe what happens to the balloon.

EXPERIMENT

You may have noticed that the balloon doesn't fully inflate. Is there a way to make it inflate more? What about if you place a bit of water in the bottle?

WHAT MAKES IT WORK

A small amount of air gets trapped inside the bottle when you cover the opening with the balloon. Air is made up mostly of oxygen and nitrogen in gas form. When the bottle is placed in the hot water, the air molecules gain energy and move further apart. When this happens they increase in volume and need more room so they push into the balloon. The opposite happens when the bottle is placed in ice water. Thermal contraction and expansion is at play here.

RE-IMAGINE IT!

What was the hardest part, and what was your plan for figuring it out?

Draw your idea here:

BUILT FROM CURIOSITY

KATHERINE JOHNSON

Katherine Johnson was born in 1918 in the rural town of White Sulphur Springs, West Virginia. From a young age, she showed an exceptional gift for mathematics and an unshakable love for numbers.

Because few schools at the time accepted Black students, Katherine's father drove her many miles each day to ensure she could attend one that did. Such discrimination in education was common in the United States during that era.

Katherine's remarkable talent and determination helped her excel academically. She graduated from high school at just 15 and completed college by 18. Through every challenge, she carried her father's wise advice: "You are no better than anyone else, and nobody else is better than you."

As a NASA mathematician, Katherine had to clearly communicate technical information under pressure. Her work was essential to the success of the Mercury and Apollo missions. Her life story, immortalized in the film *Hidden Figures*, shows how extraordinary brilliance can rise from the humblest beginnings.

DREAM BIG.

Water Gun

MATERIALS

- 16 oz water bottle (empty and dry)
- Spray nozzle from 22 oz bottle (a clean "used" or buy a cheap empty bottle from a discount store)
- Hot glue gun and glue sticks
- Craft knife

STEPS

- Glue the top of the spray nozzle to the side of the water bottle as shown
- Using the knife, make a small hole near the bottom of the water bottle along the same side as the spray nozzle. Force the end of the spray nozzle tube through the hole and hot glue around the hole to make it watertight.
- When all the hot glue has set (cooled and hardened), fill the water bottle with water. You're ready to spray!

EXPERIMENT

Adjust the nozzle tip to see how different positions affect the distance the water can travel. Try this water gun with different sizes of bottles.

WHAT MAKES IT WORK?

- A spray nozzle might look like a simple device but there's a lot of engineering at play here. When you squeeze the handle, you're using a pump to pull liquid up through the tube inside the bottle.
- Now, look closely at the tip of the nozzle. See that tiny spring? That's part of a spring and piston system. When you let go of the handle, the spring pushes it back into place—kind of like how a stretched rubber band snaps back when you let go!
- Inside the nozzle, there's also a one-way valve (called

a check valve) that makes sure the liquid only moves forward, not back down into the bottle. These parts work together to create a pressure difference.

- Here's the cool part: The inside of the nozzle has higher pressure than the air around it. When you squeeze the handle, you open a tiny passage, and the liquid rushes out to balance the pressure. This is an example of Bernoulli's principle, a rule in fluid dynamics that explains how pressure and speed are related.
- Try this experiment: Hold the nozzle close to a piece of paper and spray. Watch how the mist spreads out— that's engineering in action!
- TIP: Allow the glue to set between steps. Don't make the hole for the nozzle too big.The water bottle must have a lid.

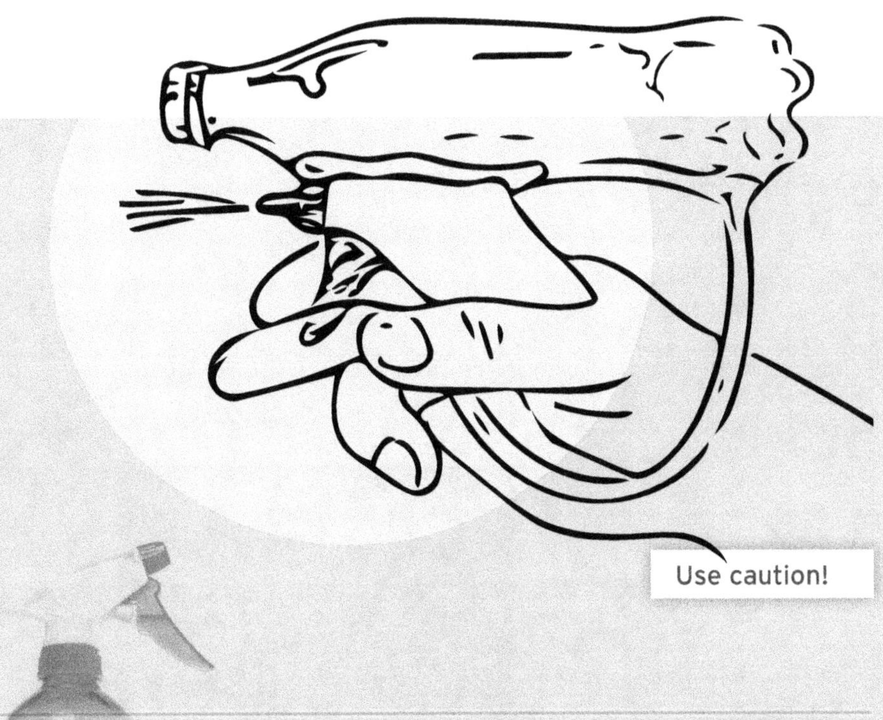

RE-IMAGINE IT!

What was the hardest part, and what was your plan for figuring it out?

Draw your idea here:

BUILT FROM CURIOSITY

LONNIE JOHNSON

As a child in Mobile, Alabama, he was known as "the Professor" for tinkering with mechanical devices; he once tore apart his sister's doll to see how it worked and tried cooking rocket fuel, nearly burning down the house. He simply loved tinkering and building contraptions. He was fascinated with science and engineering.

As a young boy, he and his friends created toys with random parts they found around the house. Later when he was a teenager, he built a compressed-air-powered robot named "Linex" and won a science fair prize.

Lonnie is best known for his invention called the Super Soaker, a popular toy water gun. He has gone on to create many other things and holds 250 patented invention. Lonnie's determination and scientific curiosity, as a young boy foreshadowed his career as an inventor and aerospace engineer. In 2022, he was inducted into the National Inventors Hall of Fame.

Lonnie's adaptability allowed him to pivot from an engineering projects to toy design.

DREAM B.G.

Plastic Bag Rope

MATERIALS
- Clean plastic grocery bags with no holes or rips
- Scissors
- Duct tape
- Cutting board (plastic or wooden; an old, heavy one works best)

STEPS

Prepare the Plastic Strips:
- Flatten the plastic bags.
- Cut them into 2-inch horizontal strips through the middle to create plastic loops.
- Connect the loops using a simple lark's head knot or another looping method. Each bag should yield about 4 to 5 loops.
- Continue linking loops until you have at least 20 to 25 feet of plastic chain.

Cut & Secure:
- Cut the looped loops into three equal sections to create strands for braiding.
- Secure the three strands to the center of the cutting board with duct tape.

Braiding the Rope:
- Arrange the three strands side by side.
- Begin braiding:
- Take the left strand and cross it over the middle.
- Take the right strand and cross it over the new middle strand.
- Repeat, alternating left and right, keeping the braid tight.

Finishing the Rope:
When finished, duct tape the ends together to form a 7-10 inch handle. Your completed rope should be almost twice the original length of your loops.

EXPERIMENT
Try cutting thinner strips—does the rope become stronger or weaker? Try braiding more strands together—how does that affect strength and flexibility?

WHY IT WORKS
You may have heard the saying, "A three-stranded cord is not easily broken." This principle applies here! Braiding distributes tension evenly, making the rope stronger and more durable than a single strand of plastic. Reusing plastic helps reduce waste.

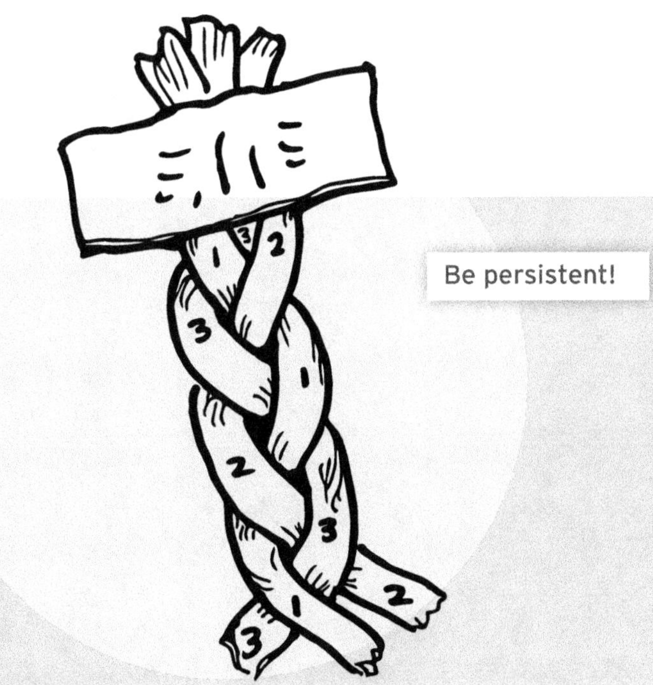

RE-IMAGINE IT!

What was the hardest part, and what was your plan for figuring it out?

Draw your idea here:

BUILT FROM CURIOSITY

LYDIA VILLA-KOMAROFF

Lydia Villa-Komaroff is a Mexican-American scientist who helped make one of the most important discoveries in biology. Born in 1947, she loved science from a young age, even though some people told her girls couldn't be scientists. She didn't listen!

Lydia studied biology and became one of the first Mexican-American women in the United States to earn a Ph.D. in science. She helped discover how to use bacteria to make insulin, a medicine that helps people with diabetes. This breakthrough has saved millions of lives!

Later, she worked as a leader in science and encouraged more young people, especially girls and students from diverse backgrounds, to follow their dreams in STEM.

Lydia Villa-Komaroff shows that with curiosity, collaboration and determination, you can change the world.

DREAM BIG.

Bin 4:
Found-items
Activities

Ping Pong Bounce

MATERIALS

- Empty egg carton (12 or 18)
- Ping pong balls (2 or more)
- Table (flat playing surface)
- Scissors or craft knife

STEPS

- Cut the top off of the egg carton
- Set the carton at one end of the table
- Bounce a ping pong ball anywhere on the empty table space between you and the egg carton. The object is to get your ball to land in an empty cell of the carton.
-

WHAT MAKES IT WORK

Cause and effect is at play here. The harder you throw your ball at the table, the higher it bounces.

EXPERIMENT

Create a game by assigning different points to each cell of the carton. For instance, portions that are further away garner the highest points. Join several empty cartons together to form a bigger game.

CAUTION

For those with egg allergies: use clean, dry yogurt cups in place of an egg carton. Tape 4-6 cups together to create your target.

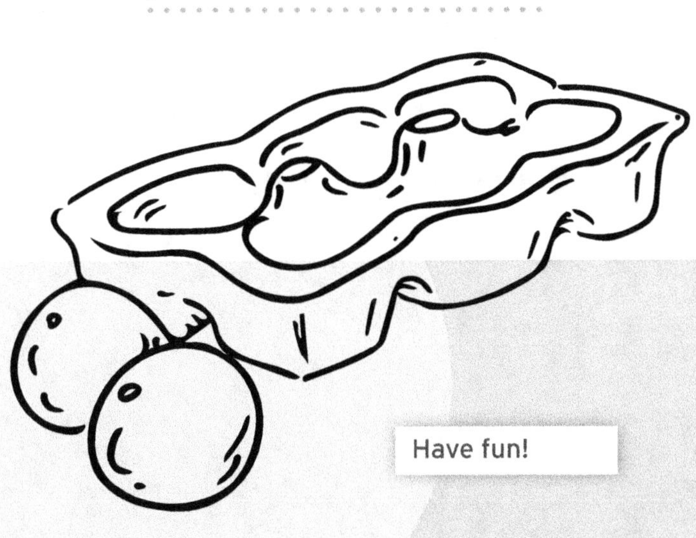

Have fun!

RE-IMAGINE IT!

What was the hardest part, and what was your plan for figuring it out?

....
....
....
....
....
....
....
....
....
....
....
....
....

Draw your idea here:

BUILT FROM CURIOSITY

CHRISTINA SOONTORNVAT

Born in 1980, Christina Soontornvat (pronounced: soon-torn-vat) grew up in a small Texas town where her family owned a Thai restaurant. When she wasn't helping out, she loved reading, dreaming up stories, and asking "how" and "why" about everything.

Her curiosity led her to study mechanical engineering, where she learned how to design and build things that work but she never stopped loving the magic of communication through storytelling. Today, Christina uses both sides of her brain: the problem-solver and the dreamer.

She's the award-winning author of books like *A Wish in the Dark* and *All Thirteen: The Incredible Cave Rescue of the Thai Boys' Soccer Team*, which blend science, adventure, and heart. Christina hopes her books inspire kids to stay curious, be kind, and remember that every question can lead to a brand-new story or discovery.

DREAM BIG.

Ping Pong Ball Chute

MATERIALS

- Ping pong balls (2 or more)
- Empty paper towel and bathroom tissue rolls (lots and lots)
- Scissors
- Painter's tape (a large roll, if possible)

STEPS

- Cut the paper towel and tissue rolls in half, lengthwise
- Tape the rolls sideways along the wall to make a chute for the balls to travel down
- Release the balls one at a time down the chute, starting at the uppermost point of the chute

EXPERIMENT

Now it's time to tinker like a scientist!

- Change the slope or height: How does that affect the speed of the ball?
- Add curves or gentle drops: Can you slow the ball down or make it stop midway?
- Race multiple balls: Which path design makes the fastest track?
- Build with a partner or team: Can you connect two sections to make a super-long chute?

WHAT MAKES IT WORK

You're seeing potential and kinetic energy at play here. It's not just a simple game; it's physics! Gravity is the 'engine' that make this chute activity compelling.

The steeper the angles you use, the faster the ball will travel down the chute. Combine intricate patterns with simple ones.

TIP FOR TEACHERS: Turn it into an engineering design challenge! Encourage them to calculate average speeds, graph results, or design the most efficient chute using principles of physics and design thinking.

RE-IMAGINE IT!

What was the hardest part, and what was your plan for figuring it out?

Draw your idea here:

BUILT FROM CURIOSITY

ROBERT H. GODDARD

Robert H. Goddard was born in Massachusetts in 1882. He came to be known as the father of modern rocketry, but his path to success was far from easy.

As a young scientist, he dreamed of sending rockets higher than anyone thought possible. Robert was often sick and spent a lot of time alone reading books. Robert's dedication to experimentation and improvement and building upon his failures is the ultimate example of a learner's mindset.

Instead of giving up, he treated every mistake as a chance to learn something new. His hard work led to the first liquid-fuel rocket, a breakthrough that opened the door to space exploration. Goddard's perseverance shows that big dreams grow when you stay curious and never stop trying.

DREAM BIG.

Newton's Compact Disc

MATERIALS

- 1 Compact Disc (CD)
- 1 marble (any color) large enough to cover the hole in the CD
- Hot glue gun (and glue stick)
- Coloring markers (at least red, green, and blue)

STEPS

- Color one side of the CD with the markers, dividing the colors equally
- Apply hot glue along the edge of the center hole
- Press the marble on the center hole, making sure the glue secures it
- Once the glue has hardened, spin the CD on a flat surface

EXPERIMENT

What happens to the colors as the CD spins? Why do you think this is going on? How does the speed of the spinning affect what you observe on the colors?

WHAT MAKES IT WORK

An optical phenomenon called additive color mixing. White light is not a single color. It's a combination of all visible colors. Every color is a different light wavelength. When all the colors are blended together at a fast pace, they look like the color white. It's color blending on a disc.

The same thing happens when you watch TV or look at pictures on a computer screen.

NOTE:
This is a great way to reuse on CDs. If you don't have a CD, cut a piece of cardboard with these dimensions: 4.7 inches (120mm) in diameter with a 9/16ths of an inch (15 mm) center hole.

RE-IMAGINE IT!

What was the hardest part, and what was your plan for figuring it out?

Draw your idea here:

BUILT FROM CURIOSITY

THEANNE GRIFFITH

Dr. Theanne Griffith has always loved asking questions about how the brain works. As a kid, she was curious about everything, from the stars in the sky to the bugs in her backyard. She also loved visiting the library as a kid and dreamed of becoming an author.

Her STEM curiosity led her to become a neuroscientist, a scientist who studies the brain and nervous system. She earned her Ph.D. and now works as a professor, discovering how our brains help us sense the world around us.

Her love of books led her to communicate through writing fun stories. Her book series, *The Magnificent Makers*, takes kids on exciting STEM adventures filled with experiments, teamwork, and imagination. Through her science and storytelling, Dr. Griffith inspires kids to stay curious, explore boldly, and believe that science is for everyone.

DREAM BIG.

Airplane Launcher

NOTE: See pages 22 and 23 for airplane-folding instructions

MATERIALS

- Chopsticks (wooden, disposable type)
- Clothespin (small wooden or plastic type, with a spring)
- Rubber bands (2)
- Craft knife or scissors
- Cutting surface

STEPS

Create the launcher:

- With the chopsticks held side by side, use one of the rubber bands to secure the clothespin to one end as shown in the diagram.
- Cut the other rubber band and tie the ends to the other end of the chopsticks as shown. This will be the trigger rubber band.
- Fold the paper airplane
- Show in pictures

Load the launcher:

- Pull the trigger rubber band back and secure it in the clothespin
- Place the finished paper airplane in the gap between the two chopsticks, with the trigger rubber band locked and loaded underneath.
- Open the clothespin and watch the airplane fly!

EXPERIMENT

Can you adapt this launcher for a bigger plane? What adjustments should you make? Bigger rubber bands? Longer sticks?

Try different airplane designs. What shapes and designs work better?

WHAT MAKES IT WORK

Potential and kinetic energy are at play here. The more energy the rubber bands can store up, the further the airplane can go.

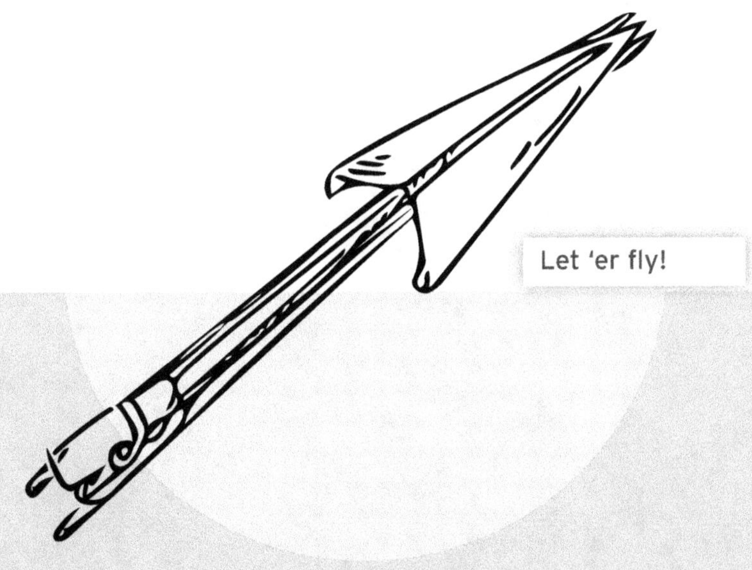

RE-IMAGINE IT!

What was the hardest part, and what was your plan for figuring it out?

Draw your idea here:

BUILT FROM CURIOSITY

BESSIE COLEMAN

Bessie Coleman was the first Black woman and the first Native American woman to become a pilot. She was born in 1892 in Texas and grew up picking cotton and helping her family.

Bessie dreamed of flying, but in the United States, flight schools wouldn't accept women or Black students. She refused to give up! She learned French, moved to France, and in 1921 earned her international pilot's license. That's an amazing achievement.

When she returned to America, Bessie became famous for her daring air shows and amazing loop-the-loop tricks. She used her fame to inspire others and to speak out against racism and unfairness.

Bessie Coleman encouraged young people, especially kids of color, to take responsiblity of their dreams and reach for the sky.

DREAM BIG.

Toothbrush Bristlebot

MATERIALS

- 1 inexpensive electric toothbrush (battery operated), with a fresh battery
- Utility knife
- Pliers
- Tape
- 3 to 4 Pipe cleaners
- Construction paper, googly eyes, etc.
- Glue

STEPS

Cut the bristle head from the toothbrush then cut the handle open and remove the motor mechanism. Set the motor aside and decorate the head with pipe cleaners and construction paper, Googly eyes, etc.

When you're done decorating the bristle part, attach the battery pack on top using tape.

Press the on/off button to turn the bot on and watch it vibrate across the table.

EXPERIMENT

Try your bot on different surfaces. Carpet. The kitchen floor. Grass. Gravel. On what surfaces does it not work? What modifications could you do to help it work on most surfaces?

WHAT'S AT WORK HERE
Friction is at play here. The motorized mechanism
generates energy as it vibrates. This energy is transferred
throughout the toothbrush, causing wobbly and
unpredictable movement across a flat surface.

REMINDER
And remember, if something doesn't work the way you
intended on your first try it doesn't mean you should give
up. Keep trying. You might discover something better.

Be persistent!

RE-IMAGINE IT!

What was the hardest part, and what was your plan for figuring it out?

Draw your idea here:

BUILT FROM CURIOSITY

DIANA TRUJILLO

Diana Trujillo is a Colombian-American aerospace engineer who helps explore Mars! She was born in Cali, Colombia, and moved to the United States when she was 17, with big dreams and little money. At first, she cleaned houses to pay for school, but she never gave up on her goal of working for NASA. After years of hard work,

Diana became one of the leaders of the Mars Perseverance Rover mission, helping scientists and engineers study the red planet. She also hosted NASA's first Spanish-language Mars landing broadcast, making space science more inclusive for millions of people.

Diana believes that anyone, no matter where they come from, can do big things through education and perseverance. This shows a strong learner's mindset.

DREAM BIG.

CD Drawbot

MATERIALS

- 1 CD (also known as a compact disc)
- 3 - 4 markers (make sure they are the same length)
- Old vibrating toothbrush
- Hot glue gun and glue sticks
- Printer paper
- Tape

STEPS

- Hot glue the bottom end of the markers to the CD, equally spaced. Make sure they glued in such a way that the CD is level and can support the toothbrush without sliding off ... show picture.
- Tape the toothbrush to the CD, lengthwise, but make sure you have access to the on/off switch.
- Take the caps off the markers and turn the toothbrush on.
- Place the DrawBot on a piece of paper and watch it draw

EXPERIMENT

Try drawing on different types of paper. Add a second or a third toothbrush to the bot. How does the additional vibration affect the function of the bot?

Vibrations!! Shaking things up is fun. In engineering design, engineers typically try to reduce the amount of vibrations because the shaking tends to damage.

Have fun!

RE-IMAGINE IT!

What was the hardest part, and what was your plan for figuring it out?

Draw your idea here:

BUILT FROM CURIOSITY

ELLEN OCHOA

Ellen Ochoa is an inspiring astronaut, engineer, and musician. The granddaughter of emigrants from Mexico, Ellen was born in 1958, in Los Angeles, California, and loved learning about science and math as a girl.

Ellen worked hard in school, earning her multiple college degrees including a doctorate in electrical engineering from Stanford. In 1993, she flew on the Space Shuttle *Discovery*, where she helped study the Earth's atmosphere. She was the first Latina to travel to space. Altogether, she spent almost 1,000 hours in space!

Later, Ellen became the director of NASA's Johnson Space Center, leading other astronauts and space missions. She's also an inventor, holding several patents for optical systems.

Ellen used a learner's mindset when sh constantly expanding her knowledge with each job. It shows she believed in continuous learning to reach her goals.

DREAM BIG.

WindMill

MATERIALS

- 1-liter plastic bottle (for the tower)
- Smaller plastic bottle (for the nacelle or cover)
- Heavy objects (marbles, rocks, or sand)
- 4 Drinking Straws (2 for the rotor, 2 for the axle)
- Paper (two 8 cm x 10 cm rectangles)
- Tape (strong clear or masking tape)
- Glue (liquid or hot glue, for paper)
- 3 Paper Clips
- String
- Small tabletop fan (for testing)

STEPS

This toy windmill is completed in 4 parts. It may take longer than other activities and may need to be completed in more than one sitting. Plan ahead.

Part 1: Building the Tower and Nacelle
- Adult Help: Have an adult cut the neck off the top of the 1-liter bottle. This is the tower base.
- Adult Help: Have the adult cut two small slots out of the sides near the top of the large bottle. This is where the smaller bottle will sit.
- Add Weight: Fill the tower base with heavy objects like marbles or rocks to stop it from falling over when the wind blows on it.
- Adult Help: Have the adult drill a hole in the cap and one in the bottom of the smaller bottle. The holes need to be slightly larger than a straw so the straw can spin freely. Alternatively, you can carefully use a soldering iron instead of a drill bit to make the holes. The holes on both ends of the bottle must be large enough for the drinking straw.

Part 2: Making the Blades and Rotor

- Make the Blades: Cut two pieces of paper, each measuring 8 cm by 10 cm. Fold each piece in half (do not crease it hard), and tape the two long edges together to form a teardrop shape.
- Connect the Rotor Straws: Pinch the end of one straw and firmly press it into the end of a second straw to connect them. Make sure this combined straw can spin freely in the holes you drilled in the smaller bottle.
- Attach the Blades: Mark a line 10 cm from each end of your connected straws. Place a thin strip of glue from the end of the straw up to that line, and hang one blade from the straw with the rounded edge facing up. Wait for the glue to dry. Repeat for the other blade.
- Curve the Blades (Pitch): Take one blade and wrap it tightly around the straw. Hold it for one minute, then let it uncurl. Do the same for the other blade, curling it in the opposite direction.

Part 3: The Axle and Lifting Mechanism

- Make the T-Clip: Bend a paper clip as straight as possible. Then, bend it into a T-shape (ask an adult for help with the pliers if you need them).
- Tape the T-Clip: Firmly tape the T-shaped paper clip to the center of your double rotor straw.
- First Axle Half: Take a third straw and slide it over the T-clip. Firmly tape this third straw to the double rotor straw; this creates the first half of your axle.
- Second Axle Half: Take a fourth straw and cut a tiny slit in one end. Straighten a new paper clip and slide it into the slit-end of the straw so a small part hangs out. Firmly tape the paper clip to the straw.
- Add the Lifting String: Cut a piece of string slightly longer than the tower. Tie one end to the paper clip you just taped to the fourth straw. Tie the other end to

a third paper clip, which you will bend slightly to use as
a hook for weights.

Part 4: Final Assembly and Testing
- Pinch the End: Take the fourth straw (the one with the
  string) and pinch and fold the open end for one minute.
  This will help it connect snugly later.
- Place the Nacelle: Place the smaller bottle (nacelle)
  horizontally into the slots at the top of the larger
  bottle (tower). Tape the two bottles together so they
  don't wobble.
- Thread and Connect: Thread the two halves of your
  axle through the holes of the small bottle. Carefully
  press the pinched end of the fourth straw into the open
  end of the third straw. Test spin the blades by hand to
  make sure the axle can spin freely.
- Test It Out! Aim a small tabletop fan at the blades and
  turn it on at the lowest speed. If it doesn't spin, move
  the fan closer or use a higher speed.
- Power Test: Hang weights (like washers) on the hook
  at the end of the string. See how much weight your
  turbine can lift at different fan speeds.

EXPERIMENT

What could you do differently with this toy windmill?
Could you make the blades larger to get it to lift a heavier
weight? How might using a used Pringles chip can be used
to create a different nacelle?

WHAT MAKES THIS WORK

The transfer of energy is at play here. Wind is basically
air in motion. It has kinetic energy. The blades (rotors)
catch that energy and this results in lift that converts this
energy to rotational energy.

The rotational (or mechanical) energy results in work being done to life the weight. There are a variety of forces involved too. For instance, the rotational force along the axle is called torque (rhymes with "mork").

Keep reading to find out about a young boy who created a real-life windmill to help his family.

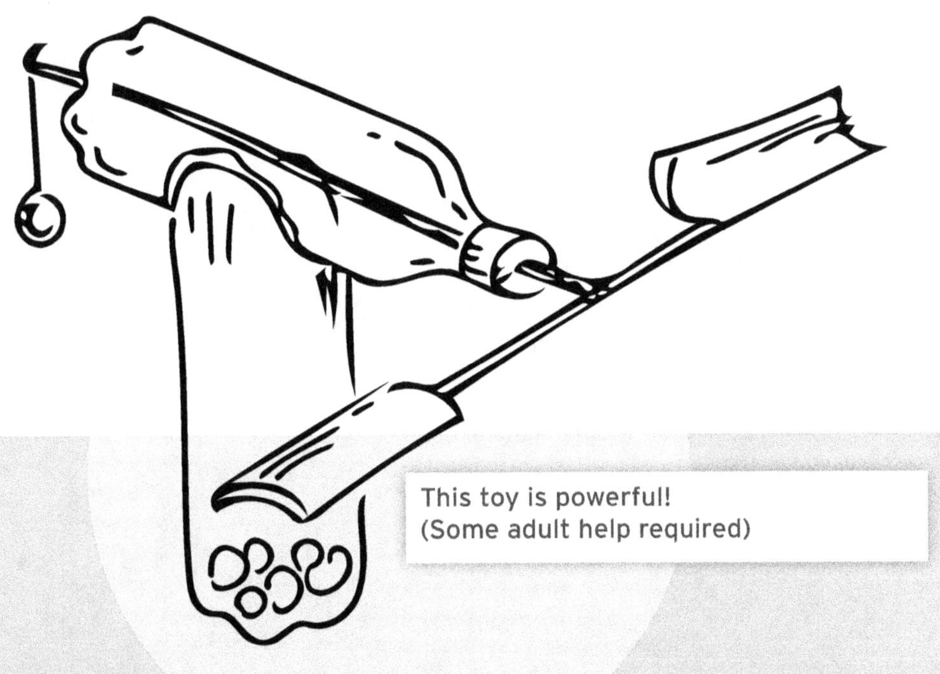

This toy is powerful!
(Some adult help required)

RE-IMAGINE IT!

What was the hardest part, and what was your plan for figuring it out?

Draw your idea here:

BUILT FROM CURIOSITY

WILLIAM KAMKWAMBA

William Kamkwamba (pronounced kam-kwom-bah) is an inventor, engineer, and author from Malawi, born in 1987. When he was a boy, a severe drought caused famine in his country, forcing him to leave school.

Despite this setback, his curiosity and love for science drove him to keep learning on his own. Using books from his local library, especially one called *Using Energy*, he taught himself about electronics and wind power. With determination and creativity, William built a windmill from scrap materials and old bicycle parts, generating electricity for his family's home and eventually for his entire village.

He later attended college, wrote a memoir, and founded the Moving Windmills Project, which helps improve lives in his Malawian community. William's story has inspired films and books, and his achievements continue to motivate young people around the world to pursue innovation, adaptability, and resilience.

DREAM B.G.

Wrapping Up

SO, WHAT DID YOU THINK OF THE WORKBOOK?

Contact us
We would like it very much if you'd send us feedback about The Dream Kit Workbook. Email us directly at idreamstem@gmail.com.
Thanks so much.

Leave a Review
If you bought this workbook on Amazon or Barnes & Noble, we would really appreciate it if you'd leave a review.
When other families see that you gained something useful from this resource, the book gets ranked higher.
We appreciate your support.

Found an Error?
If you found a mistake or something that did not quite work for you, please let us know. We are committed to publishing the best book possible.

Bulk Orders
Go Play With Junk is available to library and school systems in bulk orders, with a 75% discount. Please email idreamstem@gmail.com to inquire about orders for your library or school system.

Sources
Our online sources included like YouTube, Nasa.gov, NationalGeographic.com, and Instructables.com. All 'Built From Curiosity' images are Public Domain.

COMING TOGETHER TO ADDRESS THE PLANET'S BIG PROBLEMS

STEM professionals (scientists, technologists, engineers, and mathematicians) can make a huge difference in the world. They're helping create solutions for some of the biggest challenges humanity faces. Back in 2008, a group of top STEM experts came up with 14 game-changing goals to improve life on Earth. They named them the 14 Grand Challenges of Engineering. Since then, people all over the world have been working hard to make progress on them.

But did you know the United Nations also created a global roadmap for a better future? It's called the Sustainable Development Goals (SDGs). These 17 goals bring people, countries, and communities together to help protect our planet, end poverty, provide clean water, address climate change, and so much more. Read more about the SDGs here: https://sdgs.un.org/goals

As you move through middle school, high school, and beyond, keep these challenges and goals in mind. You can be part of the solution that helps our planet and the people on it to thrive. The world needs creative thinkers and problem-solvers from every background.

Diversity drives innovation, and every perspective helps us get closer to a sustainable, peaceful, and healthy future. So what can you imagine?

Could you be the one to invent new ways to clean the air, make water safe to drink, or design cities that work with nature? Maybe you'll help power homes with clean energy or build robots that protect coral reefs.

Every big idea starts with a curious mind like yours. Stay STEM-curious. Stay hopeful. Stay inspired. The planet needs you.

RESOURCES FOR COLLEGE-BOUND STUDENTS

College Scholarships (Partial List)

Deadlines vary. This list was compiled in 2020. Not a complete list. These scholarships are available to STEM students heading to both 2-year colleges and 4-year universities.

- Coca-Cola Scholars Foundation
- Burger King Scholars Program
- Jackie Robinson Foundation
- Blacks at Microsoft Scholarship
- Tom Joyner Foundation Scholarship
- Scholarship America
- Triangle Community Foundation
- Go Grad Scholarship
- Military Scholarship Resources
- Oppu Achievers Scholarship
- Thurgood Marshall College Fund
- United Negro College Fund (UNCF)

Various STEM Societies – with College & Professional Chapters (not a complete list):

- American Association of Civil Engineers, ASCE (https://www.asce.org/)
- Society of Women Engineers, SWE (https://swe.org/)
- National Society of Black Engineers, NSBE (https://www.nsbe.org/)
- Society of Hispanic Professional Engineers, SHPE (https://shpe.org/)
- National Society of Professional Engineers, NSPE (https://www.nspe.org/)
- IEEE (https://www.ieee.org/)
- American Association of Mechanical Engineers, ASME (https://www.asme.org/)
- American Association of Agricultural and Biological Engineers, ASABE (https://asabe.org/)
- Association for the Advancement of Medical Instrumentation , AAMI

The STEM Dreams Podcast highlighted the trials and triumphs of professionals and students in science, technology, engineering, and math fields.

Visit https://idreamstem.org/podcast to hear the episodes of past years of our podcast series

Dear Parents,

The term STEM has been around since 2001, standing for Science, Technology, Engineering, and Math. You've probably seen it on your child's schoolwork or heard about it from teachers or other parents. But what does it really mean, and why is it so important?

Science is about exploring and discovering how things work. Math helps us measure, count, and recognize patterns. Engineering combines science and math to solve problems and create innovations that make our world better. Technology ties it all together, giving us the tools to test ideas and build new solutions.

STEM learning helps children become critical thinkers, people who ask questions, analyze information, and make thoughtful decisions. These are the same skills that help young learners grow into strong leaders, no matter what career path they choose. Critical thinkers don't just build better inventions. They help build a better world.

That's why STEM education matters. It's not just about jobs or test scores; it's about preparing every child to think, create, and lead with purpose.

Join us on Facebook and Instagram
https://www.facebook.com/idreamstemdotorg
https://instagram.com/idreamstem

When you've finished the activity for the day, post it to your social media and tag us with @IDREAMSTEM and use the hashtag #goplaywithjunk

Hey, there's another workbook!

The Dream Kit Workbook is a unique 30-day STEM activity book. It combines hands-on experiments in science, technology, engineering, and math (STEM) subjects with high-impact personality spotlights written to inspire children between 10 and 12 years old to dare dream of careers in STEM. Designed by two engineers, this resource was created to require low-cost materials.

Order your copy soon. https://bit.ly/sdreamsworkbook

Email iDreamSTEM@gmail.com about bulk orders

SOURCES

The inspiration for the activities in this book came from a variety of sources. These included the following websites:

- Sciencebuddies.com
- GreenKidsCrafts
- Instructables

For a growing list of activity links, visit bit.ly/gpwj-links.